Ransomware Defense

Cisco 2nd Speci~l F~!*!~~

GW00691924

by Lawrenc~ ~~~~~

for dummies®

A Wiley Brand

Ransomware Defense For Dummies®, Cisco 2nd Special Edition

Published by
John Wiley & Sons, Inc.
111 River St.
Hoboken, NJ 07030-5774
www.wiley.com

ISBN 978-1-119-68277-6 (pbk); ISBN 978-1-119-68282-0 (ebk)

Manufactured in the United States of America

V10017296_013120

For general information on our other products and services, or how to create a custom *For Dummies* book for your business or organization, please contact our Business Development Department in the U.S. at 877-409-4177, contact info@dummies.biz, or visit www.wiley.com/go/custompub. For information about licensing the *For Dummies* brand for products or services, contact BrandedRights&Licenses@Wiley.com.

Publisher's Acknowledgments

Some of the people who helped bring this book to market include the following:

Project Editor: Elizabeth Kuball

Acquisitions Editor: Ashley Coffey

Editorial Manager: Rev Mengle

**Business Development
  Representative:** Karen Hattan

Production Editor:
  Tamilmani Varadharaj

Special Help: Rachel Ackerly, Lorraine Bellon, Scott Bower, Mary Briggs, John Damon, Tori Devereux, David Gormley, Dan Gould, Artsiom Holub, Gedeon Hombrebueno, Aivy Iniguez, Kate MacLean, Austin McBride, Ben Munroe, Mark Murtagh, Natalie Pino, Nicole Smith, Christina Soriano, Jolene Tam

Introduction

The rise of ransomware has quickly become an extremely lucrative criminal enterprise. Targeted organizations often believe that paying the ransom is the most cost-effective way to get their data back — and, unfortunately, this may be true.

In May 2019, the City of Baltimore was hit by a ransomware attack that led to chaos, leaving city officials unable to access critical infrastructure systems for over a week. Recovery from the attack was complex, costing the city an estimated $18 million — even though the criminals behind the attack only demanded $76,000 as a ransom.

But two smaller cities in Florida chose to take a different route. In June 2019, the governments of Lake City and Riviera Beach chose to pay off their attackers in exchange for the return of their data after ransomware attacks, though they still faced some work in decrypting the stolen data. The cities paid the hackers a combined $1 million in Bitcoin — and researchers say these kinds of attacks aren't going to slow down.

So, when the next city or state government gets hit, should they pay up, or start the long process of manually recovering their data? In many cases, it makes more financial sense for cities to pay the ransom and spend time decrypting their data than to spend the money to restore all their systems.

However, a study from IBM shows that American taxpayers do not support their tax money going toward paying ransomware extortion requests. The survey found that 80 percent of respondents say they're concerned about a ransomware attack on their cities, and 60 percent say they would not want their governments using taxpayer dollars to pay off attackers with the promise of returning stolen data.

The problem is that every single organization that pays to recover its files is directly funding the development of the next generation of ransomware. As a result, ransomware continues to evolve, with more sophisticated variants and more specific targeted attacks.

The costs continue to rise as well. Recent research from Cybersecurity Ventures predicts ransomware attacks will cost the global economy $6 trillion annually by 2021!

Ransomware must be prevented when possible, detected when it attempts to breach a network, and contained to limit potential damage when it infects systems and endpoints. Ransomware defense calls for a new best-of-breed architectural approach that spans the organization from the network edge of the domain name system (DNS) layer, all the way to the data center and across endpoint devices, no matter where they're being used.

About This Book

Ransomware Defense For Dummies consists of five short chapters that explore how ransomware operates and its defining characteristics (Chapter 1), security best practices to reduce ransomware risks (Chapter 2), a new best-of-breed security architecture (Chapter 3), the Cisco Ransomware Defense solution (Chapter 4), and important ransomware defense takeaways (Chapter 5).

Foolish Assumptions

It has been said that most assumptions have outlived their uselessness, but I assume a few things nonetheless!

Mainly, I assume that you know a few things about information security. Perhaps you're a C-level IT executive, IT director, senior IT architect, analyst, or manager, or a security, network, or system administrator. As such, this book is written primarily for technical readers who know a little something about IT networking, infrastructure, and enterprise systems.

If any of these assumptions describes you, then this book is for you! If none of these assumptions describes you, keep reading anyway. It's a great book, and when you finish reading it, you'll know enough about ransomware defense to be dangerous (to the bad guys)!

Icons Used in This Book

Throughout this book, I use special icons to call attention to important information. Here's what to expect:

REMEMBER

This icon points out information that you should commit to your nonvolatile memory, your gray matter, or your noggin — along with anniversaries and birthdays!

TECHNICAL STUFF

You won't find a map of the human genome here, but if you seek to attain the seventh level of NERD-vana, perk up! This icon explains the jargon beneath the jargon and is the stuff legends — well, nerds — are made of!

TIP

Thank you for reading, hope you enjoy the book, please take care of your writers! Seriously, this icon points out helpful suggestions and useful nuggets of information.

WARNING

This icon points out the stuff your mother warned you about. Okay, probably not. But you should take heed nonetheless — you might just save yourself some time and frustration!

Beyond the Book

There's only so much I can cover in 48 short pages, so if you find yourself at the end of this book, thinking, "Gosh, this was an amazing book. Where can I learn more?," just go to `https://umbrella.cisco.com/how-to-stop-ransomware`.

Chapter **1**

What Is Ransomware?

Ransomware is one of the fastest-growing malware threats today and is already an epidemic. According to research from Cybersecurity Ventures, a new organization will fall victim to ransomware every 14 seconds in 2019, and every 11 seconds by 2021. In this chapter, you learn about ransomware — what it is, how it's evolving as a threat, and how it works.

Defining Ransomware

Ransomware is malicious software (malware) used in a cyberattack to encrypt the victim's data with an encryption key that is known only to the attacker, thereby rendering the data unusable until a ransom payment (usually *cryptocurrency,* such as Bitcoin) is made by the victim.

TECHNICAL STUFF

Cryptocurrency is an alternative digital currency that uses encryption to regulate the "printing" of units of currency (such as Bitcoin) and to verify the transfer of funds between parties, without an intermediary or central bank.

Ransom amounts are typically high, but usually not exorbitant. For example, demands for individuals typically range from $300 to $600, while larger organizations will typically pay more. This characteristic of ransomware is, by design, in an effort to get victims to simply pay the ransom as quickly as possible, instead of contacting law enforcement and potentially incurring far greater direct and indirect costs due to the loss of their data and negative publicity. However, these amounts are increasing over time, as attackers begin to focus their attention on organizations with higher capacities to pay larger amounts (and more to lose). The average ransom demand by hackers to release files encrypted by their ransomware attacks has almost doubled in 2019 to over $12,000, based on cases handled by cybersecurity company Coveware.

WARNING

Ransom amounts may also increase significantly the longer a victim waits. Again, this is by design, in an effort to limit a victim's options and get the victim to pay the ransom as quickly as possible.

Recognizing Ransomware in the Modern Threat Landscape

Ransomware is not a new threat. The earliest known ransomware, known as PC Cyborg, was unleashed in 1989. Since that time, ransomware has evolved and become far more sophisticated. Ransomware has also become more pervasive and lucrative with developments such as the following:

>> **Ongoing digital transformation:** As more organizations digitize their operations and employees use email, cloud apps, and mobile devices to get work done, the number of potential entry points for attackers increases exponentially. After a network has been breached, infections can spread more quickly when critical systems are connected.

>> **The rise of cryptocurrency:** Currency (such as Bitcoin) enables easy and virtually untraceable payments to anonymous cybercriminals. As cryptocurrency speculation continues to push prices higher, the potential for large ransoms grows proportionally.

>> **The emergence of Ransomware-as-a-Service (RaaS):** *RaaS* (ransomware that can be purchased for a small fee and/or a percentage of the ransom payment) makes it easy for practically anyone to use ransomware.

Despite sensational media reports about massive data breaches targeting organizations and enterprises such as the U.S. Office of Personnel Management (OPM), Equifax, Target, Home Depot, and Capital One, in terms of cyberattacks, the rise of ransomware has become one of the most pervasive threats to organizations and enterprises — as well as individuals.

WARNING

A report by Kaspersky suggests that 34 percent of businesses hit with ransomware took a week or more to regain access to their data. What would you do if your organization was in the dark for a week?

Locky is one example of an aggressive ransomware variant. In 2016, it was compromising as many as 90,000 victims per day. At that time, the average ransom for a Locky attack was usually between 0.5 and 1 Bitcoin. Based on statistics from Cisco's Talos threat intelligence group, on average, 2.9 percent of compromised victims in a ransomware attack would pay the ransom. In that case, Locky would potentially infect as many as 33 million victims over a 12-month period, resulting in between $287 million and $574 million in ransom payments (see Table 1-1).

TABLE 1-1 **Estimate of Locky Total Ransom Payments**

Ransom Price	1 Bitcoin	0.5 Bitcoin
Victims/day	90,000	90,000
Number of payouts/day	2,610	2,610
Bitcoin price (October 2, 2016)	$610.82 = 1 Bitcoin	$610.82 = 1 Bitcoin
1-day profits	$1,594,240	$797,120
1-month profits	$47,826,206	$23,913,603
12-month profits	$573,926,472	$286,963,236

Although a conservative estimate of $287 million may seem trivial in comparison to even a single data breach (such as the 2013 Target data breach, which is estimated to have cost Target over $300 million), it's important to remember that data breach loss estimates are based on costs to the organization that is targeted, not the individual victims whose identities and/or credit card information is stolen. Costs to the organization include the following:

>> **Regulatory fines and penalties** levied by various regulatory bodies, such as the Payment Card Industry (PCI)

>> **Legal fees** associated with litigation resulting from the breach

>> **Loss of business** due to business interruptions, brand reputation damage, and loss of customers

>> **Remediation** including incident response and recovery, public relations, breach notifications, and credit monitoring services for affected individuals

TIP

The Ponemon Institute reports that the average cost of a data breach to an organization in 2019 is $3.92 million, an increase of 12 percent from 2014.

Meanwhile, Locky was still active in 2018, when the price of Bitcoin had increased by *over ten times* — on October 2, 2018, a single Bitcoin was worth over $6,500! With no upper limit on the prices of cryptocurrency, it's easy to see that ransomware has the potential to be a major financial burden for any targeted organization.

Cybercriminals typically sell stolen credit card and identity information on the *dark web* — anonymous web content (such as black market drug sales, child pornography, cybercrime, or other activities attempting to avoid surveillance or censorship) that requires special software, configuration, and/or authorization for access — for as little as a few cents to several dollars per record. By comparison, a cybercriminal can make several hundred dollars to tens of thousands of dollars from ransoms directly paid to them by individual victims and organizations.

The actual cost to victims of identity theft and credit card fraud was estimated in Javelin Strategy and Research's *2016 Identity Fraud Study* to be $15 billion in 2015. Follow-up research indicated that the rate of identity theft and credit card fraud has continued to drop, from $8.1 billion in 2017 to $6.4 billion in 2018. Although identity theft and credit card fraud are in decline (likely due to stronger card security measures), many other cyberattacks —

including ransomware — are on the rise. Research from Accenture indicates that nearly $5.2 trillion of combined value could be at risk globally from cyberattacks from now through 2023.

As ransomware attacks continue to cause greater economic impacts, the patterns of attacks are changing, too. Instead of holding individuals and small businesses for ransom, attackers are moving toward "quality over quantity." A study by F-Secure found that instead of casting a wide net, more attackers are using specific targeting to increase the chances of a large payout. As an example, Ryuk ransomware payments are typically much higher than the average ransomware payout. This is due to the highly targeted nature of Ryuk attacks on medium-to-large organizations with a greater ability to pay.

Ransomware vectors are changing, too. In the past, criminals would send large numbers of phishing emails, hoping that a few unlucky people would respond and expose their networks to ransomware attacks. Now, more ransomware variants are leveraging vulnerabilities in remote desktop protocols to enter the network, taking advantage of unpatched systems and zero-day exploits.

Understanding How Ransomware Operates

Ransomware is commonly delivered through exploit kits, *waterhole attacks* (in which one or more websites that an organization frequently visits is infected with malware), *malvertising* (malicious advertising), or email phishing campaigns (see Figure 1-1).

TIP

Go to `https://learn-umbrella.cisco.com/product-videos/ransomware-anatomy-of-an-attack` to see the anatomy of a ransomware attack.

| Infection Vector | C2 Comms and Asymmetric Key Exchange | Encryption of Files | Ransom Demand |

FIGURE 1-1: How ransomware infects an endpoint.

Once delivered, ransomware typically identifies user files and data to be encrypted through some sort of an embedded file extension list. It's also programmed to avoid interacting with certain system directories (such as the WINDOWS system directory, or certain program files directories) to ensure system stability for delivery of the ransom after the payload finishes running. Files in specific locations that match one of the listed file extensions are then encrypted. Otherwise, the file(s) are left alone. After the files have been encrypted, the ransomware typically leaves a notification for the user, with instructions on how to pay the ransom (see Figure 1-2).

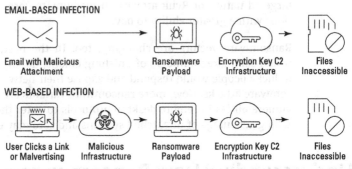

EMAIL-BASED INFECTION

Email with Malicious Attachment → Ransomware Payload → Encryption Key C2 Infrastructure → Files Inaccessible

WEB-BASED INFECTION

User Clicks a Link or Malvertising → Malicious Infrastructure → Ransomware Payload → Encryption Key C2 Infrastructure → Files Inaccessible

FIGURE 1-2: How ransomware works.

WARNING

There is no honor among thieves. Although an attacker will usually provide the decryption key for your files if you pay the ransom, there is no guarantee that the attacker hasn't already installed other malware and exploit kits on your endpoint or other networked systems, or that they won't steal your data for other criminal purposes or to extort more payments in the future.

Chapter **2**

Implementing Best Practices to Reduce Ransomware Risks

I n this chapter, I review security best practices and risk mitigation strategies that, if fully and correctly applied, will help your organization effectively defend against ransomware and other cybersecurity threats.

Before an Attack: Discover, Enforce, Harden

The MITRE Corporation, a nonprofit government advisory agency, believes that offense is the best driver for defense against cyber-attacks, particularly when strong offense and defense teams work together. There are, of course, a number of best practices that organizations can proactively implement before they're ever targeted by an attacker. If attackers can't easily establish an initial foothold — get their foot in the door, so to speak — they'll likely seek an easier victim, unless your organization is the object of a targeted attack.

Ransomware attacks can be opportunistic — the attacker's motive is often profit, with as little risk and effort as possible. So, preventing an attacker from gaining entry to your network with an architectural approach is the most effective way to prevent a ransomware attack from succeeding in the first place.

REMEMBER

The MITRE ATT&CK matrix is a framework that describes tactics, techniques, and procedures used by attackers at various phases to gain access to systems and launch cyberattacks. The ATT&CK categories are, in order:

>> Initial Access

>> Execution

>> Persistence

>> Privilege Escalation

>> Defense Evasion

>> Credential Access

>> Discovery

>> Lateral Movement

>> Collection

>> Command and Control (C2)

>> Exfiltration

>> Impact

The first six categories are all focused on gaining access to the target's network and systems.

Attackers usually achieve initial access to a target through one of three methods:

>> Social engineering/phishing to get an unsuspecting user to expose network credentials or install malware

>> Using legitimate credentials that have been stolen or sold, often exposed via a data breach

>> Exploiting a vulnerability in a public-facing (Internet) application or service

WARNING

In the 2019 Data Breach Investigations Report, Verizon found that users are much more vulnerable to social attacks that they receive on mobile devices. There are two reasons:

>> Mobile devices are small, and user interfaces make it difficult to evaluate whether an email or web page is legitimate.

>> People are often using their mobile devices while walking, talking, driving, and doing other activities that limit their ability to pay close attention.

TIP

The following best practices should be implemented to prevent attackers from gaining access to your organization's network and systems:

>> **Conduct regular security awareness and training for your end users.** This training should be engaging and contain the latest information on security threats and tactics. Be sure to do the following:

● Reinforce company policies regarding not sharing or revealing user credentials (even with IT and/or security), strong password requirements, and the role of authentication in security (including the concept of *nonrepudiation,* which gives users the "It wasn't me!" defense).

● Encourage the use of company-sanctioned Software-as-a-Service (SaaS) applications, such as file-sharing programs, to exchange documents with others rather than email attachments, as a way to mitigate (or completely eliminate) phishing attacks containing malicious attachments.

● Consider non-native document rendering for PDF and Microsoft Office files in the cloud. Desktop applications such as Adobe Acrobat Reader and Microsoft Word often contain unpatched vulnerabilities that can be exploited.

● Instruct users who do not regularly use macros to never enable macros in Microsoft Office documents. A resurgence in macro-based malware has been observed recently that uses sophisticated obfuscation techniques to evade detection.

● Explain incident reporting procedures and ensure that users feel comfortable reporting security incidents with messages like "You're the victim, not the perp" and "The cover-up is worse (in terms of damage) than the event."

- Remember to cover physical security. Although they're less common than other forms of social engineering, visitor escort policies and tactics such as dumpster diving, shoulder surfing, and piggybacking (or tailgating), which potentially threaten their personal safety as well as information security, should be reiterated to users.

>> **Perform ongoing risk assessments to identify any security weaknesses and vulnerabilities in your organization, and address any threat exposures to reduce risk.** Be sure to do the following:

- Conduct periodic port and vulnerability scans.

- Ensure solid and timely patch management.

- Disable unnecessary and vulnerable services and follow system hardening guidance.

- Enforce strong password requirements and implement two-factor authentication (where possible).

- Centralize security logging on a secure log collector or security incident and event management (SIEM) platform, and frequently review and analyze log information.

TECHNICAL STUFF

In the past, most ransomware required some form of user interaction, such as opening an email attachment or clicking a malicious link, or involved taking advantage of unpatched systems. But some ransomware variants don't need help from a user to launch an attack. The Sodinokibi ransomware variant used a recently disclosed vulnerability in Oracle WebLogic to download ransomware to an affected server and launch an attack, before a patch could be released to stop it.

Unfortunately, despite your best efforts, people are people (and Soylent Green is people!) and there will always be zero-day threats that exploit previously unknown — and therefore, unpatched — vulnerabilities. If an attacker succeeds in accessing your network, his next step is to establish C2 communications, in order to

>> Ensure persistence

>> Escalate privileges

>> Move laterally throughout your network, data center, and end user environment

To mitigate the effects of a successful intrusion, implement the following best practices:

>> Deploy domain name system (DNS) layer protection that enables you to predictively identify malicious domains, IP addresses, and Internet infrastructure to help mitigate the risk of an attack.

>> Automatically enable firewall, advanced malware protection, encryption, and data loss prevention on all endpoints, including personal mobile devices (if "bring your own device" [BYOD] is permitted) and removable media (such as USB drives) that is transparent to the user and requires no action by the user. This protects roaming and remote users both on and off the network, even when they don't necessarily do what they're supposed to do with regard to best practices and established policies.

>> Enable security functionality on email gateways including blocking or removing executables and other potentially malicious attachments, sender policy framework (SPF) verification to mitigate email spoofing, and email throttling (or "graylisting") to rate-limit potential spam emails.

>> Enable security products and services that analyze Internet traffic, emails, and files to prevent infection and data exfiltration (discussed further in Chapters 3 and 4), and leverage threat intelligence services for deeper context and rapid investigation.

>> Design and deploy a robust, inherently secure security architecture that uses segmentation to restrict an attacker's lateral movement in your environment.

>> Enforce the principle of least privilege and eliminate user "privilege creep" to limit an attacker's ability to escalate privileges.

>> Regularly back up critical systems and data, and periodically test backups to ensure they can be restored and are good. Also encrypt your backups and maintain them offline or on a separate backup network.

>> Assess and practice your incident response capabilities, and monitor and measure the overall effectiveness of your security posture on an ongoing and continual basis.

TIP

Most ransomware relies on a robust C2 communications infrastructure, for example, to transmit encryption keys and payment messages. By preventing an attacker from connecting with ransomware that has infected its network, an organization can stop a successful ransomware attack. If, for example, the attacker is unable to send encryption keys to an infected endpoint or instruct a victim on how to send a ransom payment, the ransomware attack will fail. As Table 2-1 shows, many ransomware variants rely heavily on DNS for C2 communications. In some cases, a Tor (The Onion Router) browser is also used for C2 communications. Therefore, it's important to be able to block both types of communications, using a method like a proxy.

TABLE 2-1 **C2 Communications Examples in Ransomware**

Name	Encryption Key	Payment Message
Locky	DNS	DNS
TeslaCrypt	DNS	DNS
CryptoWall	DNS	DNS
TorrentLocker	DNS	DNS
PadCrypt	DNS	DNS, Tor
CTB-Locker	DNS, Tor	DNS
FAKBEN	DNS	DNS, Tor
PayCrypt	DNS	DNS
KeyRanger	DNS, Tor	DNS

During an Attack: Detect, Block, and Defend

If your organization is under attack, fast and effective incident response is required to limit any potential damage. The specific action steps and remediation efforts to be undertaken will be different for each unique situation. However, the time to learn the breadth and extent of your organization's incident response capabilities is not during an attack! Your incident response efforts should be well understood and coordinated — which is accomplished before an attack — and well documented and repeatable, so that you can reconstruct an incident after an attack and identify lessons learned and potential areas for improvement.

A key component of effective incident response that is often overlooked is information sharing, which includes the following:

» **Communicating timely and accurate information to all stakeholders:** Pertinent information needs to be provided to executives in order to ensure adequate resources are committed to response and remediation, critical and informed business decisions can be made, and appropriate information is, in turn, communicated to employees, law enforcement, customers, shareholders, and the general public.

» **Automatically sharing new security intelligence throughout the architecture:** Bringing together critical data from disparate systems such as SIEM, threat intelligence, and sandboxing tools enables the incident response team to quickly surface and effectively triage high-impact security incidents. For example, if a new malware payload is detected on an endpoint, it should automatically be sent to a cloud-based threat intelligence platform for analysis in order to find and extract any indicators of compromise (IoCs). Then new countermeasures should automatically be deployed and enforced.

After an Attack: Scope, Contain, and Remediate

Important actions after an attack has ended include the following:

TIP

» Resuming normal business operations, including restoring backups and reimaging systems, as necessary

» Collecting and preserving evidence for law enforcement and auditing purposes

» Analyzing forensic data to predict and prevent future attacks, for example, by identifying related domains and malware with the associated IP addresses, file hashes, and domains

» Performing root cause analysis, identifying lessons learned, and redeploying security assets, as necessary

Predictive threat intelligence enables a proactive security posture by enabling your organization to see the C2 infrastructure that attackers are leveraging for current and future attacks, and thereby always stay ahead of the threat.

Chapter **3**

Building the New Best-of-Breed Security Architecture

I n this chapter, you learn about various challenges in current approaches to security architecture, and a new best-of-breed architecture to better address modern threats, including ransomware.

Recognizing the Limitations of Current Security Designs

In the past, many businesses thought they had to make a choice when it came to security:

» They could use best-of-breed products that were effective against specific types of emerging threats but did not fully integrate into an architectural approach to integrating defenses.

>> They could take a systems approach that assimilated standalone (or point) security products that were "good enough" into an intelligent system architecture.

Many organizations today have deployed a hierarchical network architecture consisting of an access, distribution, and core layer with multiple standalone security products, deployed in a DMZ or local services zone, such as a firewall and/or web proxy server. Unfortunately, this is not the same thing as true "defense in depth" (see Figure 3-1).

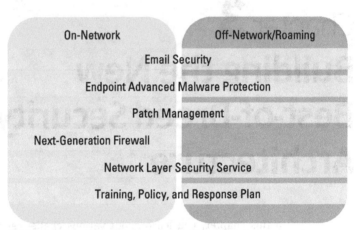

FIGURE 3-1: Security is about managing risk through layers.

Limitations with current approaches include the following:

>> **There's no integration or correlation.** Too many stand-alone security products inevitably inundate limited security resources with verbose, uncoordinated information that can't be easily analyzed and leaves security teams looking for the proverbial "needle in a haystack."

>> **Perimeter-based security is only one part of an effective architecture.** Firewalls, secure web gateways, and sandboxing technology deployed at the network edge only see north–south traffic traversing the Internet. East–west traffic in the data center (traffic between applications and end users that never traverses the Internet) can account for as much as 80 percent of all network traffic — so complete visibility across the entire network is needed.

» Employees have left the building. Not only have cyber-criminals changed the way they work (their tactics and techniques), but the way in which our users work and interact digitally has also changed. With more remote and roaming on-the-go users working directly via the cloud on various devices, perimeter-based security technologies and virtual private networks (VPNs) are no longer able to fully protect devices and corporate data. Many cloud-based services (such as Salesforce.com and Office 365) can be conveniently accessed without a VPN connection, leaving these applications and data with only basic security, such as antimalware protection. According to Enterprise Strategy Group, 79 percent of organizations are moving to direct Internet access (DIA) at remote office locations, bypassing traditional perimeter security appliances and leaving users at risk for attacks. Modern security solutions need to enable your business to embrace the cloud and work from any device, anywhere, at any time — extending existing protection well beyond the traditional network perimeter.

» There's a lack of visibility. Traditional port-based firewalls are blind to many threats that use evasive techniques such as nonstandard ports, port hopping, and encryption.

» There isn't enough segmentation, and traditional segmentation can be challenging. Networks are commonly segmented into "trusted" and "untrusted" zones with static virtual LANs (VLANs) defined on switches, which can be hard to configure and maintain. This arbitrary structure doesn't address the new normal in modern data centers — virtual machines (VMs) that move dynamically throughout and across data centers and in the cloud. Instead, multiple granular segmentation (including micro-segmentation) needs to be defined on network devices throughout the data center with dynamic software-defined segmentation.

» Static updates are only a starting point. Downloading and installing anti-malware signature files is only a starting point for effectively fighting today's rapidly evolving zero-day threats. How can you protect against zero-day and unknown threats, and how prepared are you to defend against previously benign files that suddenly become malicious? Static signature files need to be bolstered with real-time, cloud-based threat intelligence and a more dynamic and continuous security approach — for the riskiest 1 percent of attacks that can lead to costly breaches.

Defining the New Best-of-Breed Security Architecture

To safeguard businesses against ransomware and other modern threats, a new best-of-breed security architecture leverages an integrated, portfolio-based approach that is simple, open, and automated, rather than traditional point products. This new architecture

>> Automatically shares threat intelligence and provides aggregated, correlated context with other security products and services, both on premises and in the cloud

>> Reduces complexity and provides full visibility across the entire environment

>> Allows better integration with new and existing security investments using open, extensible standards and technology

>> Uses integration to deliver automated security response, so security becomes more effective and reduces the burden on other IT teams

What does this mean for your business? This new best-of-breed security architecture uncovers more threats faster, and allows for better remediation and prevention going forward. A platform-based approach provides you with the contextual awareness you need to connect the dots between threat signals that may be missed when analyzed by themselves. It also helps threat hunters to understand not only what threats are inside their environments, but how they got there in the first place — and prevent others from getting inside.

This architecture consists of the following components (see Figure 3-2):

>> Next-generation firewalls (NGFWs) and next-generation intrusion prevention systems (NGIPSs) with visibility into intrusion events, with data enrichment from other security products

- » Threat intelligence from industry-leading sources and cloud-based product data, with the ability to collect and prioritize high-urgency incident data for further investigation and response

- » Domain name system (DNS) layer security to extend protection beyond the organization's firewalls

- » Secure web gateway to protect across all ports and protocols

- » Cloud access security broker (CASB) to protect against risky, unauthorized cloud apps

- » Highly granular, software-defined network segmentation with role-based policy enforcement regardless of location, device, or IP address

- » Email, web, and endpoint security to expand visibility and correlate threats

- » Advanced malware protection with sandboxing capabilities from the network to the endpoint

- » Automated platform integrations, along with centralized visibility and management, to tie components together and make life easier for your security operations team

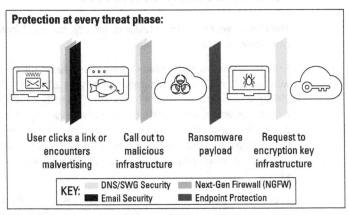

Protection at every threat phase:

User clicks a link or encounters malvertising   Call out to malicious infrastructure   Ransomware payload   Request to encryption key infrastructure

KEY: DNS/SWG Security   Next-Gen Firewall (NGFW)
Email Security   Endpoint Protection

FIGURE 3-2: The new best-of-breed security architecture provides the best threat surface coverage possible with defense in depth.

TIP

In Chapter 4, you learn about Cisco's approach to this new best-of-breed security architecture with Cisco Ransomware Defense. Figure 3-3 maps out the Cisco Security products that prevent, detect, and respond to ransomware attacks.

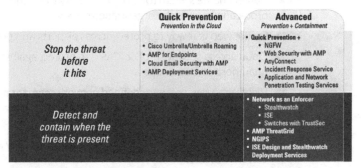

FIGURE 3-3: Cisco Ransomware Defense solution bundles available.

NHL UNIVERSITY PROTECTS ITS STUDENTS AND FACULTY FROM CYBER THREATS

The challenge: Protecting students, faculty, and staff from ransomware attacks

NHL University is one of the top-ranking universities in the Netherlands, with more than 12,000 students and more than 1,200 staff. In February 2016, just as exams were about to start, the university was threatened by a ransomware attack. After the initial ransomware attack left them vulnerable, additional cyberattacks were launched on their network, threatening their most critical systems. The ongoing attacks left NHL administrators wondering if they would even be able to go ahead with exams.

But with the help of Dimension Data and Cisco, NHL was able to address their crisis and improve their security stack. They deployed Cisco Umbrella to provide security protection at the DNS level for all devices and users, no matter where they went on campus. Later, NHL added Advanced Malware Protection (AMP) across the 1,900 supported devices within their network for additional protection against malware infections. With their new security architecture in place, the exams went ahead on schedule. But that was just the beginning.

The solution: Deliver a complete security solution with the help of trusted advisers

With students, faculty, and staff using their own devices on campus, NHL knew that they needed to understand what security issues were taking place on their network and what to do about them. After starting to deploy their new security solutions, they realized that they needed help from experts to accelerate time-to-value, train staff quickly, use all the functionality in the right way, and connect the tools in their systems to track key performance indicators (KPIs). To get that help, NHL engaged with the Cisco adoption team. Together, NHL and Cisco hosted workshops to focus on opportunities and solve security pain points.

After deploying Cisco Umbrella, the next task was to successfully implement AMP technology to protect endpoints on the NHL network. Since adding Cisco Umbrella and AMP to their security stack, NHL has experienced no further ransomware issues. After that initial success, the Cisco adoption team also helped NHL to develop dashboards to monitor and measure activity on its networks, as well as deliver reports to senior management to reassure them that threats were being blocked earlier. Finally, the Cisco team helped NHL to develop processes and workflows to proactively take steps to prevent attacks in the future.

The impact: Gaining network visibility and intelligence, and preparing for the future

The adoption journey together didn't end there. In 2018, NHL merged with Stenden Hogeschool to form a new multi-campus university: NHL Stenden University. It was double the size — 25,000 students and 2,250 staff across ten sites all around the world — which means a lot of potential new threats. In partnership with Cisco, NHL reviewed its security architecture across the entire university system and made significant investments in software and hardware to improve its security posture ahead of the merger.

With the increasing number of ransomware attacks taking place in the world, it's only a matter of time until major universities are chosen as high-profile targets. But now, NHL Stenden University is ready to face the challenge.

Chapter 4

Deploying Cisco Ransomware Defense

C isco Ransomware Defense offers an integrated approach that provides protection from ransomware for all office locations and users, even when off the virtual private network (VPN). Backed by unmatched threat intelligence from Cisco Talos, Cisco's unified architecture brings together complementary security products including domain name system (DNS), web, email, endpoint, and network security. In this chapter, you learn about the Cisco Ransomware Defense solution and why Cisco's solutions deliver the most effective protection against ransomware from the network to email, and the endpoint to the cloud.

TIP

It may seem like there are a lot of tools in this list. The good news is, you don't have to log into each one and manage them separately! Cisco Threat Response automates integrations across many Cisco security products and aggregates their intelligence sources into an integrated platform. This gives you greater visibility and context so you can investigate and remediate security activities easily across your environment.

Protecting Against Ransomware, Starting with DNS

There are many phases in a ransomware attack. Before launching an attack, the attacker needs to stage Internet infrastructure to support the execution and command-and-control (C2) phases. Cisco Umbrella stops ransomware attacks (and other cyberattacks) earlier by blocking Internet connections to malicious sites serving up ransomware in the first place. Built into the foundation of the Internet, Umbrella enforces security at the DNS and Internet Protocol (IP) layers (see Figure 4-1).

Cisco Umbrella can also be integrated with Cisco SD-WAN to provide additional layers of protection against ransomware attacks for direct Internet access breakouts at satellite offices. These additional controls include secure web gateway, cloud-delivered firewall, and cloud access security broker (CASB) functionality, delivered from a single cloud-native platform.

TECHNICAL STUFF

SD-WAN stands for Software-Defined Wide Area Networking.

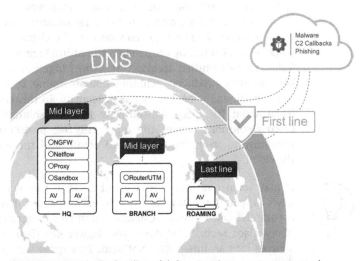

FIGURE 4-1: DNS is the first line of defense against ransomware attacks.

Unlike appliances, the cloud service protects endpoints both on and off the corporate network. Unlike agents, DNS layer protection extends to every device connected to the network — easily.

It's the fastest way to protect all your users, and it can be deployed in as little as 30 minutes.

TIP

To learn more, download the *Umbrella Advantage* e-book at https://learn-umbrella.cisco.com/ebooks/the-umbrella-advantage-what-makes-cisco-umbrella-unique.

CISCO IT IMPLEMENTS UMBRELLA TO DEFEND AGAINST RANSOMWARE AND OTHER RESIDENT EVILS

Beginning in April 2016, Cisco adopted Umbrella for its internal IT with two primary goals:

- **To increase protection against malware, botnets, and breaches:** As a global DNS provider network, Umbrella sees 2 percent of the world's Internet requests. It quickly learns about and blocks emergent threats before they have a chance to do harm.

- **To gain insights about risky user behavior:** Umbrella generates a log showing all activity on the Internet, regardless of port and protocol. The logs give Cisco's security and IT teams increased visibility and audit capabilities.

Transitioning to Umbrella was exceptionally simple. "We added powerful new controls without needing to deploy new hardware, reconfigure the network, conduct extensive interoperability testing, or change any of our other systems," says Rich West, Cisco Information Security (InfoSec) architect.

Cisco formed an eight-member team from IT and InfoSec to plan and implement Umbrella. The technical aspects of the transition took very little time. The team members spent most of their time meeting with application owners and network operations teams to explain the benefits of the transition and to answer any questions related to potential impacts to application or network performance.

The conversion was as simple as adding four lines of code to the DNS configuration file on Cisco's internal DNS servers to direct que-

(continued)

ries to Umbrella. Now Cisco IT's DNS servers ask Umbrella for recursive DNS queries instead of asking their upstream neighbors. The conversion was so seamless that internal users didn't even know a change had occurred.

Cisco Umbrella unifies multiple security services into a single cloud platform to secure Internet access and control cloud app usage from your network, branch offices, and roaming users. Before users connect to any online destination, Umbrella acts as a secure onramp to the Internet and delivers deep inspection and control to support compliance and block threats. Umbrella also provides interactive access to threat intelligence to aid in incident response and threat research.

HOW A GLOBAL MEDICAL MANUFACTURER ROUTS OUT RANSOMWARE

The challenge: Fighting infinite security challenges with finite resources

In the decades since its 1983 founding, Octapharma has steadily become one of the world's largest human protein manufacturers. With a corporate initiative designed to double production capacity and increase overall efficiencies now underway, however, the company is experiencing unprecedented expansion.

The impact of this growth spurt is evident throughout the organization — even at the network level. "As we add more employees in more locations using more mobile devices and cloud services, we also add new network security vulnerabilities," says Octapharma Global Senior Network Engineer Jason Hancock. "We've seen a spike in a variety of malicious activities, including ransomware."

"Rather than trying to cover any exposures by hiring the kind of trained security practitioners already in short supply, identifying new solutions to address those vulnerabilities and aligning with organization efficiency objectives has been a priority," he adds.

"In keeping with that focus," says Hancock, "first we needed to keep the network from going down every 15 minutes and improve efficiencies both for our team and users. When I joined the company in 2014, my initial objective was to get things stabilized so I could focus on preventing incrementally more aggressive malware, such as a CryptoLocker breach that we encountered."

The solution: Functionality that fits

"Before I came to Octapharma, the team had been working for some time to migrate from on-premises web security appliances to the same vendor's cloud service, selected by a predecessor. I was initially tasked with completing that deployment," recalls Hancock. "As soon as I saw what I was being asked to work with, I knew it wasn't going to meet our needs."

"We encountered significant issues that caused concern as to the product's viability in our environment, starting with Internet functionality." Notes Hancock, "Our team received a lot of feedback from users who were dissatisfied with Internet service, which was attributed to both the cloud service and the endpoint client on users' machines."

"Outside of that," he continues, "the feature set was inconsistent with our needs and there was widespread difficulty throughout the team around administration. This meant we had to provide a lot of training to support very detailed, nonintuitive management of policies and various components."

"After an issue-laden North American deployment, our network was down on a regular basis. The unreliability of having no Internet for hours at a time reflected unfavorably on our team, and was not resolvable through the product's support channels," Hancock explains. "Finally, [the vendor] suggested we abandon our migration to the cloud in favor of virtual appliances, which required redirection of traffic from more than 50 global locations, which was undesirable and in some cases not possible."

"That's when I raised my hand and said, 'the only way to solve this problem is Cisco Umbrella, and I can have it deployed and protecting our global network within six weeks.' After investing so much in a solution that didn't work for us, we were ready for a solution I knew from previous experience would succeed: Umbrella."

(continued)

(continued)

The results: Drastic reduction in ransomware

After an easy deployment, Octapharma saw immediate results. "Since we put Umbrella in place, we've had no web security compromises," Hancock says.

"We have drastically reduced our exposure to ransomware, and since deploying Umbrella, we have not been a victim of ransomware as a result of clicking a malicious link. We actually see tens of thousands of blocks per week due to security policy; that doesn't count blocks based on category policies," he adds. "We have covered a great risk in the web attack vector of ransomware, and greatly improved our user experience in regards to Internet connectivity."

"We've even identified a few phishing emails and tested them by trying to click on their links; thanks to Umbrella, the sites were not accessible."

Another unexpected benefit? Says the network engineer, "By correlating the great data that comes out of the Umbrella dashboard with our internal systems, we've found infected machines that were previously undetected."

With its security stack now able to block threats at the DNS layer, the firm continues to look for ways to keep reinforcing the network with proactive security management. "While Umbrella is very capable of blocking sites based on category policies, it's most effective as a security tool and with that as a focus in our deployment, it's a critical component of our defense-in-depth strategy. I'm currently investigating additional tools that are part of Cisco's security portfolio to continue bolstering that strategy," the network engineer notes. "I am considering firewall enhancements, malware protection for endpoints, and greater coordination among the products in our security toolset."

For Jason Hancock, seeing has always been believing. "I've been using Umbrella at home for years," he says. "And now that I've seen it succeed in two different organizations as well, my colleagues tell me that they too just can't say enough about Cisco's unique and highly effective approach to security."

Securing Endpoints and Addressing Email Threats

Today's malware threats are more sophisticated than ever. Advanced malware, including ransomware, evolves quickly and can evade detection after it has compromised a system using various methods, including the following:

» Sleep techniques
» Polymorphism and metamorphism
» Encryption and obfuscation
» Use of unknown protocols

At the same time, advanced malware provides a launching pad for a persistent attacker to move laterally throughout a compromised organization's network.

Email phishing campaigns are a favorite — and astonishingly effective — malware attack vector for cybercriminals. Common ransomware variants use phishing techniques to infect their victims.

Cisco Ransomware Defense solutions secure endpoints and prevent email threats, and include Cisco Advanced Malware Protection (AMP) for Endpoints and Cisco Cloud Email Security with AMP.

Cisco Advanced Malware Protection for Endpoints

Traditional antimalware software that only uses point-in-time detection techniques alone will never be 100 percent effective. Yet, it takes only one threat that evades detection to compromise your entire environment. Using targeted context-aware malware, sophisticated attackers have the resources, expertise, and persistence to outsmart point-in-time defenses. Point-in-time detection is also completely blind to the scope and depth of a breach after it happens, rendering organizations incapable of stopping an outbreak from spreading or preventing a similar attack from happening again.

TIP

Although no antimalware solution can remove ransomware or decrypt files once an endpoint is infected, Cisco helps organizations proactively detect ransomware and block it before it ever reaches the network.

Based on this understanding of malware, Cisco created AMP for Endpoints to deliver a complete framework of detection capabilities and big data analytics to continuously analyze files and traffic in order to identify and retrospectively block advanced malware threats at the first sign of malicious behavior. Sophisticated machine-learning techniques evaluate more than 400 characteristics associated with each file. Advanced search allows you to know everything about the endpoint, dramatically accelerating security investigations. *Retrospective security* — the ability to look back in time and trace processes, file activities, and communications in order to understand the full extent of an infection, establish root causes, and perform endpoint isolation and other forms of blocking and remediation techniques — can detect and alert you to files that become malicious after the initial disposition. This combination of continuous analysis and retrospective security provides advanced malware protection that goes beyond traditional point-in-time detection (see Figure 4-2).

FIGURE 4-2: Point-in-time detection compared with continuous analysis and retrospective security.

Cisco Email Security with Advanced Malware Protection

Email is a critical business communication tool, but it can expose organizations to a broad range of sophisticated threats. Cisco Email Security with AMP blocks spam, phishing emails, malicious attachments, and URLs, which are important attack vectors for ransomware. The AMP technology is the same that is applied on the endpoint, but it is deployed at the email gateway.

Cisco Email Security with AMP protects business–critical email with layered protection that includes

- ❯❯ Global threat intelligence
- ❯❯ Spam blocking
- ❯❯ Graymail detection and safe unsubscribe
- ❯❯ Advanced malware protection

CISCO DRINKS ITS OWN CHAMPAGNE

Cisco IT relies on the Cisco Email Security with AMP for its threat-centric email security strategy. The following graphic shows how Cisco Umbrella, Cisco AMP for Endpoints, and Cisco Email Security with AMP work together to stop ransomware attacks in different ways.

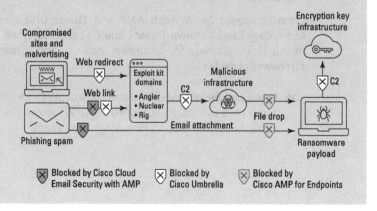

- Outbreak filters
- Web interaction tracking
- Outbound message control
- Forged email detection
- Data loss prevention

Protecting the Network with Next-Generation Firewalls and Segmentation

Cisco Firepower threat-focused next-generation firewalls (NGFWs) deliver an integrated threat defense across the entire attack continuum — before, during, and after an attack — with unparalleled visibility not possible in legacy port-based firewalls. Cisco TrustSec technology delivers dynamic software-defined network segmentation. It uses the existing network for granular role-based security policies to be enforced on discrete network segments, regardless of the user's location or device. The outcome is simpler segmentation that helps prevent malware from moving laterally within an organization's network; this can limit malware damage once a breach has occurred.

Cisco Firepower Next-Generation Firewall

Cisco Firepower NGFW with AMP and Threat Grid sandboxing technology blocks known threats and C2 callbacks while providing dynamic analysis for unknown malware and threats. Cisco Firepower provides

- **Precise application visibility and control (AVC):** Identify and control user access to more than 4,000 commercial applications, plus support for custom applications.

- **>> Cisco Next-Generation IPS:** Highly effective threat prevention and a full contextual awareness of users, infrastructure, applications, and content help you detect multi-vector threats and automate defense response.

- **>> Reputation- and category-based URL filtering:** This filtering provides comprehensive alerting and control over suspect web traffic. It enforces policies on hundreds of millions of URLs in more than 80 categories.

- **>> Advanced malware protection:** Effective breach detection with low total cost of ownership (TCO) offers protection value. Discover, understand, and stop malware and emerging threats missed by other security layers — activated with a simple software license.

Use the network as a sensor and enforcer

Cisco uses the network to dynamically enforce security policy with software-defined segmentation designed to reduce the overall attack surface, contain attacks by preventing the lateral movement of threats across the network, and minimize the time needed to isolate threats when detected.

Cisco solutions enable the network itself to act as a sensor and enforcer. Identity Services Engine (ISE) with TrustSec and Stealthwatch simplifies the provisioning and management of secure network access, provides greater visibility into anomalous network activity, accelerates security operations, and consistently enforces policy anywhere in the network. Unlike access control mechanisms, which are based on network topology, Cisco TrustSec controls are defined using logical policy groupings, so resource segmentation and secure access are consistently maintained, even as resources move in mobile and virtualized networks. What does all this mean? TrustSec policy enforcement can prevent a ransomware attack from spreading throughout your network.

REMEMBER

Cisco TrustSec functionality is embedded in Cisco switching, routing, wireless LAN (WLAN), and firewall products to protect assets and applications in enterprise and data center networks.

Traditional access control methods segment and protect assets using virtual LANs (VLANs) and access control lists (ACLs). Cisco TrustSec instead uses security group policies, which are written in a plain-language matrix and decoupled from IP addresses and VLANs. Users and assets with the same role classification are assigned to a security group.

Cisco TrustSec policies are centrally created and automatically distributed to wired, wireless, and VPN networks so that users and assets receive consistent access and protection as they move in virtual and mobile networks. Software-defined segmentation helps reduce the time spent on network engineering tasks and compliance validation.

Streamlining Deployments and Bolstering Incident Response

Cisco Security Advisory Services include deployment services for Cisco Ransomware Defense solutions including Firepower and AMP, as well as incident response.

The Cisco Security Services Incident Response team can provide

>> Proactive incident response readiness services to help your organization develop and/or evaluate its incident response capabilities

>> Reactive incident response in the case of a ransomware attack or other security incidents

Additionally, Cisco Security Integration Services address solution-level architectural challenges. It streamlines the deployment of solution technologies like Cisco AMP for Endpoints and Firepower NGFWs.

REMEMBER

These components form the foundation of the Cisco Ransomware Defense approach. But you can improve your security posture across all parts of your organization with even more solutions from Cisco. Explore the entire Cisco security portfolio at www. cisco.com/c/en/us/products/security.

PERFORMANCE WITH CISCO

The challenge: Developing defense-in-depth protection

Prologis, Inc., the global leader in logistics real estate, leases modern distribution facilities to a diverse base of approximately 5,200 customers across two major categories: business-to-business and retail/online fulfillment. It has 60+ offices in 20 countries on four continents.

"Being global means working everywhere, and being able to do so successfully means a heavy reliance on cloud computing," says Prologis Security Solutions Architect, Tyler Warren. "Since the majority of Prologis's IT infrastructure is in the cloud, we don't have a typical infrastructure or perimeter, which can make identifying security solutions difficult."

As a publicly-held, cloud-centric, global organization, Prologis needs to protect its systems from being compromised, and making sure that doesn't happen by building out its security stack is Warren's mission.

"As we saw threat activity increase, it became clear that Prologis needed to fortify existing security measures to protect the network and safeguard users on and off network against malicious activity such as command-and-control callbacks, malware, and phishing," he continues. "A layered security model made sense for us, because no single security element is strong enough to catch everything."

The solution: Strengthened security that fits the stack and staff

"Building out our security stack took some trial-and-error. We wanted all the elements to be compatible and capable of being seamlessly integrated with no impact to users. And," Warren notes, "they had to protect us where we work: everywhere in the world and in the cloud."

Prologis's short blocklist of very specific offensive content types required web filtering, which was handled initially by another vendor. According to Warren, "We found it hard to manage. More important, it didn't fit with our corporate goal of moving everything to the cloud."

"We needed a security layer that could help us combat certain security issues raised by employee Internet usage, and we also needed to step up our web filtering," he recounts. "We appreciated the fact that Umbrella is the first layer to block malicious activity."

(continued)

(continued)

In the search for the best way to meet those needs, Prologis ran proof-of-concept trials with three other vendors, and Cisco. After eliminating the others based on a variety of factors including hardware requirements, complexity, time-intensive setup, and price, Prologis chose Cisco Umbrella.

"Umbrella meets all our needs," Warren says. "It addresses our specific security concerns, takes care of web filtering, and it covers our remote users — all in a single cloud-based, easily deployed solution."

The results: Policy enforcement with dramatic performance gains

"We didn't have to wait long to see results," states Warren. "The ability to consistently enforce policies everywhere — including off-network devices — is hugely important to Prologis," he adds. "The Umbrella roaming client implementation was so seamless that no one is even aware it's engaged."

Warren points to a significant boost in performance as yet another positive outcome. "After we installed Umbrella, we saw a huge improvement in performance. Since the majority of the apps Prologis uses are in the cloud, performance is extremely important to us. One hundred percent of the apps we use experienced performance gains."

Other Umbrella features have proven useful as well. "Automated reporting is valuable — especially the Cloud Services Report — because I'm able to share clear, digestible data about how well the network is protected and how much shadow IT is happening in the cloud, which has been a real eye-opener," Warren notes. "The reporting makes it easy for me to identify any issues, and makes a lot of people's lives better by underscoring the need for our defense-in-depth security infrastructure."

"Adding Umbrella to our security stack has been a great decision. Everyone is ecstatically happy about the improved security and performance we've experienced as a result of its deployment."

Chapter **5**

Ten Key Ransomware Defense Takeaways

n this chapter, I cover some important points about ransomware defense that are well worth remembering!

Ransomware Is Evolving

Ransomware is a rapidly evolving threat. Ransomware is a rapidly evolving threat. Recent research from Cybersecurity Ventures predicts that a new organization will fall victim to a ransomware attack every 11 seconds by 2021, and new variants are being developed all the time! This makes defending your organization's data against ransomware more critical than ever before.

As ransomware attacks continue to cause greater economic impacts, the patterns of attacks are changing to "quality over quantity." This is possible due to more highly targeted attacks, using ransomware variants like Ryuk, on medium to large organizations with a greater ability to pay.

Several factors have contributed to the rapid growth and evolution of ransomware, including digital transformation initiatives (which greatly increases the number of potential entry points and the ability for attacks to propagate), the rise of Bitcoin (enabling easy and virtually untraceable payments to cybercriminals), and the emergence of Ransomware-as-a-Service (RaaS; see the next section), which makes it easy for practically anyone to use ransomware.

Ransomware-as-a-Service Is an Emerging Threat

RaaS has emerged as a new threat that literally makes it as easy as "one, two, three" for practically anyone with limited technical skills to become a cybercriminal. For example, Tox — one of the earliest known RaaS offerings, first discovered in May 2015 — can be downloaded from the dark web using a Tor browser and then set up as follows:

1. Enter a ransom amount.
2. Create a ransom note.
3. Type a CAPTCHA so that the creators of Tox know you're not a bot.

RaaS software is typically available to download for free or for a small fee. The real profit for the creators of RaaS software is in the cut they take of the ransom payments that are collected — typically from 5 percent to 30 percent.

Paying a Ransom Doesn't Solve Your Security Problems

For most victims of ransomware, the quickest and easiest way to deal with the problem is simply to pay the ransom. However, paying the ransom — although you may get access to your files — doesn't necessarily solve your problems.

In most cases, your files will be decrypted if you pay the ransom, but there's no guarantee. Although it's in the cybercriminals' best interests to restore your files if you pay the ransom (if a ransomware campaign gains a reputation for not decrypting files when the ransom is paid, then there is no reason for future victims to pay the ransom), there's no honor among thieves. This is particularly true with the emergence of RaaS because a "newbie" cybercriminal may not see the bigger picture. Also, if the encryption key doesn't work for some reason, you can't just call customer service!

There's also no guarantee that the perpetrator didn't install other malware or exploit kits to facilitate future cyberattacks against your organization. A copy of your files may also have been exfiltrated for other purposes, such as selling your organization's sensitive information on the dark web.

Paying a ransom directly funds and perpetuates future cybercrime. It's exactly the same thing as paying a ransom to terrorists or rogue nation-states in exchange for hostages. It emboldens, encourages, and finances similar acts in the future.

Finally, paying a ransom doesn't negate the fact that a serious security breach has occurred in your organization. Depending on the nature, scope, and circumstances of the breach, and the industry regulations and legal jurisdictions that your organization is subject to, you may be required to publicly disclose the breach and pay severe fines and penalties — kind of a slap in the face after already paying a ransom!

TIP

To mitigate potential damage from a ransomware attack, organizations should always ensure they maintain periodic, known good backups of all important files and current images of all critical systems.

Build a Layered Security Architecture Based on Open Standards

Open and extensible standards enable a new best-of-breed architecture that allows new and existing security technologies to be easily integrated into a comprehensive security solution.

Deploy Integrated, Best-of-Breed Solutions

Defense in depth is a long-established security industry best practice. Unfortunately, until now, defense in depth has required organizations to deploy standalone (or point) security products that don't integrate easily with other security solutions in the environment.

With the new best-of-breed architecture, organizations can deploy integrated portfolio-based solutions that reduce complexity in their security environment and improve their overall security posture.

Embed Security throughout Your Network Environment

Security must be inherent and pervasive throughout the organization's entire computing environment, including across the network, throughout the data center, on endpoints and mobile devices, and in the cloud.

Reduce Complexity in Your Security Environment

Security technologies should be simple to deploy and use. Complexity introduces risk due to the possibility of misconfigurations and errors, and can potentially bury important indicators of compromise (IoC) and other data points in cumbersome and verbose logs. To pull together an integrated security plan and eliminate unnecessary complexity, don't hesitate to lean on third-party security services and leverage their breadth of experience in order to complement your own in-depth knowledge and understanding of your organization's environment and threat posture.

Leverage Cloud-Based, Real-Time Threat Intelligence

Ransomware and other cybersecurity threats are evolving rapidly. Zero-day attacks represent the greatest threat to most organizations. Cloud-based, real-time threat intelligence enables IT teams to deploy the most up-to-date countermeasures as quickly as possible when new threats emerge, and leverage security expertise that extends well beyond their organization.

Automate Security Actions to Reduce Response Time

Wherever possible, security actions should be automated to keep pace with threats that can spread throughout an entire enterprise network within minutes or seconds.

Here are some examples of security actions that can be automated:

>> Distribution and installation of antimalware and intrusion prevention system (IPS) signature files

>> Centralized collection, correlation, and analysis of security logs and threat data

>> Threat protection that blocks requests to malicious destinations before a connection is even established and stops threats over any port before they reach your network and endpoints

>> Dynamic access control lists (ACLs), domain and website whitelisting/blacklisting, and firewall rule creation

>> Account provisioning/deprovisioning and access rights management

See Something, Say Something

The U.S. Federal Bureau of Investigation (FBI) is urging ransomware victims to report their infection details, which will in turn give the FBI a more comprehensive view of ransomware's spread and impact. The FBI says it has been challenging "to ascertain the true number of ransomware victims as many infections go unreported."

The FBI is concerned that victims are not reporting infections for a number of reasons — one main reason being that victims don't see the point in doing so, especially if they resolve the issue internally either by paying the ransom or cleaning the malware infection.

REMEMBER

The FBI doesn't advocate paying a ransom. "Paying a ransom does not guarantee the victim will regain access to their data," according to the FBI. "In fact, some individuals or organizations are never provided with decryption keys after paying a ransom. Paying a ransom emboldens the adversary to target other victims for profit, and could provide incentive for other criminals to engage in similar illicit activities for financial gain."

TIP

To report an infection, go to www.ic3.gov and provide the following:

>> Date of infection and victim company information (such as industry type and business size)

>> Ransomware variant (identified on the ransom page or by the encrypted file extension)

>> How the infection occurred (for example, a link in an email, browsing the Internet)

>> Requested ransom and amount paid (if any)

>> Attacker's Bitcoin Wallet address (may be listed on the ransom page)

>> Overall losses associated with a ransomware infection (including the ransom amount and victim impact statement)